What most people don't understand is that UFOs are on a cosmic tourist route. That's why they're always seen in Arizona, Scotland, and New Mexico. Another thing to consider is that all three of those destinations are good places to play golf. So there's possibly some connection between aliens and golf.

Alice Cooper

We have over 500,000 illegal immigrants living in Arizona. And we simply cannot sustain it. It costs us a tremendous amount of money of course in health care, in education, and then, on top of it all, in incarceration. And the federal government doesn't reimburse us on any of these things.

Jan Brewer

I look at my grandparents and what they dealt with in the Japanese internment in Arizona. That sense of perseverance, of making the best out of an incredibly bad situation, has always been something I drew inspiration from. I always ask myself, 'What in the world do I have to complain about?'

Scott Fujita

America is the only developed nation that has a 2,000-mile border with a developing nation, and the government's refusal to control that border is why there are an estimated 460,000 illegal immigrants in Arizona and why the nation, sensibly insisting on first things first, resists 'comprehensive' immigration reform.

George Will

Baseball, it is said, is only a game. True. And the Grand Canyon is only a hole in Arizona. Not all holes, or games, are created equal.

George Will

The strike of the miners in Arizona was one of the most remarkable strikes in the history of the American labor movement. Its peaceful character, its successful outcome, were due to that most remarkable character, Governor Hunt.

Mary Harris Jones

I flew into New York for the Raising Arizona audition, and we just started joking around.

John Goodman

Despite Arizona's remarkable growth in recent years, we have met the current federal health standards for ozone pollution and the Environmental Protection Agency recently approved our dust control plan.

Jane D. Hull

There's not a single person in Arizona today who would say the Grand Canyon was a mistake.

Stewart Udall

It wouldn't matter whether you were Latino or Hispanic or Norwegian. If you didn't have proof of citizenship and if the police officer had reasonable suspicion, he would ask and verify your citizenship. I mean, that's the way that it is. That's what the federal law says. And that's what the law in Arizona says.

Jan Brewer

I was honored to wear 'Arizona' across my chest. I am extremely blessed to have my education completely paid for and take part in the great tradition of Wildcat softball. To have my jersey number retired was the ultimate compliment.

Jennie Finch

And you know, it's not just illegal immigration. Terrorists can come across. They're devastating our ranchers down in southern Arizona - drop houses, kidnapping, automobile accidents, extortion, drugs, the spill-over with the drug cartels. We're facing all of it.

Jan Brewer

Arizona presents no specific reason for excepting capital defendants from the constitutional protections extended to defendants generally, and none is readily apparent.

Ruth Bader Ginsburg

We have serious enemies and growing threats around the world. Unfortunately, we have an administration whose idea of a rogue state is Arizona.

Mitt Romney

Prescott National Forest is right on the edge of my home in Arizona.

Maynard James Keenan

I have been coaching recently. I coached high school basketball in Arizona, and I hope that more opportunities become available.

Kareem Abdul-Jabbar

If Democrats start consistently winning Arizona, New Mexico, Colorado and Nevada, the electoral outlook for Republicans in the future is mighty bleak.

Mark McKinnon

I was raised in Arizona, and I went to public school, and the extent of my knowledge of the civil-rights movement was the story of Rosa Parks and Martin Luther King, Jr. I wonder how much my generation knows.

Emma Stone

I spend most of hunting season at the ranch. We all love to hunt whitetails, and we have a pretty good supply in South Texas. I also love to hunt elk in Arizona, mule deer in Utah, and I've been to Canada to hunt caribou.

George Strait

Arizona's law makes what is already a federal offense - being in the country illegally - a state offense. Some critics seem not to understand Arizona's right to assert concurrent jurisdiction.

George Will

I speak as much Spanish as anyone who has grown up in Southern California or Texas or Arizona. I had my three years of high-school Spanish and a couple of semesters in college.

Will Ferrell

Arizona, our beautiful state, was built on mining. Copper is huge here, and now uranium. And then we have the federal government coming in, writing all these rules and regulations and telling us that we can't do this and we can't do that. We need concise, clear answers.

Jan Brewer

I had a brief experience in the food industry. I was a bus boy in a Mexican restaurant in Arizona, scraping re-fried beans off people's plates. It teaches you a bit of humility and the importance of a good deodorant.

Wentworth Miller

You don't go to Gettysburg with a shovel, you don't take belt buckles off the Arizona.

Robert Ballard

Fifty thousand people in Mexico have been murdered. Puerto Penasco, 60 miles south of our border, just had five people and a police officer killed. That is like part of Arizona, and it is spilling over into our state.

Jan Brewer

I think what's going to hurt the Republicans enormously is the extremist position of Mitt Romney on the immigration issue and states like New Mexico, states like Colorado, Nevada, Arizona - and I think it's going to be the margin of victory for President Obama, a very narrow victory.

Bill Richardson

I went to the University of Arizona. I stopped because I went there for two years and I felt like I experienced college or whatever. I'm over it. I like Hollywood better.

Nicole Richie

These smugglers, many of them present in trafficking through my State of Arizona, create false Social Security cards, false green cards, visas and a variety of other fraudulent documents as an essential part of their smuggling activities.

John Shadegg

President Obama has decided to have the United Nations review the law of Arizona. You have got to be kidding! We're now going to have countries like Cuba, Libya and Uganda sitting in judgment on Arizona's laws? Enough is enough!

Russell Pearce

My very first job was a cashier at Burger King in Tucson, Arizona. And I occasionally worked the drive-thru. I'd go wherever I was needed! My second job was at Dairy Queen. I stayed in the fast food royalty.

Kate Walsh

But the people of Arizona, the people of America, have been promised that our borders would be secured for years and years and years, with it not happening. And I don't believe the people of America, certainly not the people of Arizona, are ready to discuss anything other at this point in time other than securing our borders.

Jan Brewer

Well, I think it's real important that people understand, first and foremost, those of us that have lived in Arizona or in southern California, we have a very diverse population. The Hispanic population has been part of all of our lives since we've been born here or since we've grown up here.

Jan Brewer

I lived on a farm with cows, and I lived in the city with rats. My family stayed in Colorado for a while, then went from Los Angeles to Arizona. People would ask me where I'm from, and I would have to say, 'I don't have a clear answer for you.'

Jason Behr

We have at least 125 communities in Arizona at risk from wildfire, not because of review processes or litigation delays but because of a lack of federal funding on the ground to actually begin the projects.

Janet Napolitano

I knew Arizona's SB 1070 would be controversial when I introduced it, but I did not expect the national immigration debate to revolve around a state law. While the anti-American open-borders Left attack me and the law as 'racist,' 'nativist' and their other empty smear words, the vast majority of the people of Arizona and America support the law.

Russell Pearce

The murder of Robert Krentz - whose family had been ranching in Arizona since 1907 - by illegal alien drug dealers was the final straw for many Arizonans. But there are dozens and dozens of other citizens of our state who had been murdered by illegal aliens. Currently 95 illegal aliens are in Maricopa County jail for murder.

Russell Pearce

When Maricopa County Arizona Sheriff Joe Arpaio cracked down on illegal immigration without getting permission from Obama, they threatened to revoke his 287(g) status. When Sheriff Joe refused to balk, they filed suit against him with a frivolous civil rights claim.

Russell Pearce

We can't have - we can't have a patchwork of 50 states developing their own immigration policy. I understand the frustration of people in Arizona. They want the federal government to step up and deal with this problem once and for all, and that's what we want to do.

David Axelrod

Governor Jan Brewer and the Arizona legislature have created an environment in Arizona where performing is no longer a neutral act. They have created an environment where they can convert the normal commercial interaction between artists and their fans into the means to apply this racist law.

Zack de la Rocha

Racial discrimination is illegal. It's illegal in the United States. It's illegal in Arizona. It has been and it will continue to be.

Jan Brewer

Arizona, our beautiful state, was built on mining.

Jan Brewer

So if Arizona sees the federal government isn't assuming its responsibilities, it creates local laws. But migration and keeping security on the borders is not a local or state issue, it's a federal issue.

Vicente Fox

I am encouraged that there's going to be much better dialogue between the federal government and the state of Arizona. I mean, I hope that's not wishful thinking.

Jan Brewer

Arizona's forest fires are not waiting for April, and neither will we. That is why I am pushing for stepped up deployment for Hot Shot wildfire crews in March rather than April, in order to better prepare for the expected fires in northern Arizona.

Rick Renzi

My wife used to be an anchorwoman in Arizona, so she knew John McCain, and she liked him, and I kinda liked him.

Clint Eastwood

Anytime that the Arizona Cardinals play football, I scream at the top of my lungs at the television. And I have certain dances that I do.

Blake Shelton

Arizona is a national leader in school choice with both charter schools and tuition tax credits giving parents and their children more school choices than ever before.

Jane D. Hull

I care very much about women and their progress. I didn't go march in the streets, but when I was in the Arizona Legislature, one of the things that I did was to examine every single statute in the state of Arizona to pick out the ones that discriminated against women and get them changed.

Sandra Day O'Connor

Arizona is gorgeous. The sunshine in Arizona is gorgeous red.

Cecilia Bartoli

I majored in journalism at Arizona State University, where I began writing the columns I write now, but I cannot, in good conscience, refer to myself as a writer. I'm a columnist, maybe a journalist, I guess I'm an author, but writer... no. That's not up to me to call myself, that's rather lofty. It's for the reader to decide.

Laurie Notaro

I think it's really cool, but Jimmy Eat World and Gin Blossoms did it better than anyone. People don't realize just how awesome the Arizona history is, especially for alternative music. Growing up, that's all I ever wanted to be was those two bands.

Nate Ruess

Arizona is really cool but I couldn't stay there for too long.

Dar Williams

The United States and Arizona are both losing jobs to offshore locations.

Janet Napolitano

Arizona has become a national leader in the restoration of the Rule of Law, with over 100,000 illegal aliens having left the state since 2007.

Russell Pearce

Out of labor's struggle in Arizona came better conditions for the workers, who must everywhere, at all times, under advantage and disadvantage work out their own salvation.

Mary Harris Jones

I remember when I was a young social worker, the first time I went to the state capital in Arizona, where I eventually served for seven years, I was so nervous to go and lobby my state legislators. Because I only had a master's degree at the time in social work.

Kyrsten Sinema

It's rewarding to be recognized by the fans and other players for my abilities and to be able to represent the Arizona Cardinals fans from around the world.

Larry Fitzgerald

Producing fuel cells and solar panels requires high tech facilities and produces high paying jobs. The industry is booming in Arizona. The state already has about 100 firms in the solar industry and has grown 20% since 2003.

J. D. Hayworth

The point at which we worked with some of these actors, they weren't really stars yet. Nicolas Cage was not a big star when we did Raising Arizona. A lot of these people were also virtually unknown, too, when we worked with them first.

Joel Coen

I have always aspired towards other people's looks. When I was young, I loved teddy boys; I thought they looked wonderful. Then I was a cowboy in Arizona, really for the clothes! I had a ranch for five years; I had chaps made of bearskin.

Nicholas Haslam

I would rather be known as 'Jim Kolbe, the trade expert in Congress who happens to be gay,' rather than 'Jim Kolbe, gay congressman from Arizona.'

Jim Kolbe

Arizona faces unique healthcare challenges including uncompensated care for illegal immigrants, and the large number of Native Americans who live in remote and isolated areas of the state.

Rick Renzi

As a little girl in Arizona, none of the women in my family had a cultural connection with Girl Scouts, but the opportunity resonated with my mother as a platform that would allow me to excel in school.

Anna Maria Chavez

For example, in my own State of Arizona, an Israeli scientist is working with an Arizona company on a demonstration project involving a very fast-growing algae which can be used to power a biomass energy plan.

John Shadegg

I am Hualapai. We are located in Northern Arizona, at the Grand Canyon. We own the Skywalk area.

Kiowa Gordon

I supported Arizona's immigration law by joining in that lawsuit to defend it. Every day I have Texans on that border that are doing their job.

Rick Perry

I have a home in Arizona. I go a couple months a year, but basically Chicago is my home.

Dennis Farina

I love design in general, the creativity. Whether it is golf courses, my apparel line, ads we do or our business with AriZona, design is fun.

Jack Nicklaus

I took an oath to protect the people of Arizona, and that's what I'm going to do. I'm going to keep pushing in that direction.

Jan Brewer

Arizona is now recognized as a premier place in which to locate, expand and grow a business.

Jan Brewer

When states like Alabama and Arizona passed some of the harshest immigration laws in history, my Attorney General took them on in court and we won.

Barack Obama

I often say that Arizonans should decide what's best for Arizona.

Jane D. Hull

Sarah Palin is brilliant. She is a media magnet and a media magnate. She creates headlines and draws crowds wherever she goes, whether it's 98 degrees in the desert of Arizona or below freezing in the snow of Wisconsin.

Mark McKinnon

Arizona now has one of the most innovative systems of financing school construction in the nation.

Jane D. Hull

Arizona faces many challenges ahead. None is more important or more pressing than passing a new state budget.

Jane D. Hull

I also want to thank Arizona citizens for their efforts at conserving energy last summer.

Jane D. Hull

Today, Arizona's sons and daughters, mothers and fathers are proudly serving their country.

Jane D. Hull

For a border state, I would argue that Texas is less lunatic on the subject of immigration issues than other places around it, like Arizona. They're much more comfortable with their long-term identity as a place with a very large Hispanic population.

Gail Collins

I worked at a movie theater in Tempe, Arizona, when I went to community college there. And I got fired because a sorority had rented out a theater to watch 'Titanic,' and they were being really rude to me while they were waiting for the movie. So as I tore their tickets, I told them the end of the movie.

Bill Hader

The attack and our response show just how vital Arizona's military bases are to the defense of our country. We need to do everything we can to protect them.

Jane D. Hull

Arizona is a red state, and we're going to keep it red.

Jan Brewer

Arizona has always been anti-black.

Paul Mooney

I divide my time between homes in Arizona and England, six months a year in each place.

Terri Windling

I first saw the ocean as a kid. We would drive from Arizona in the summer and arrive as the sun was starting to come down over the hill near Laguna in southern California. We would always sing a song, and it was a big joyous family moment when we came over the hill.

Ted Danson

I grew up in Flagstaff, Arizona, without a television or any connection with pop culture. My father was a director of a museum and research center. Many of my friends were Hopi kids, which meant I'd go to their villages and mesas. They'd pray and dance to their gods the way they'd been doing for hundreds of years. So I was blessed with tolerance.

Ted Danson

Arizona is the worst place to spend the summer - it's like 125 degrees - so my mom, my brother and I would go to the beach for two months to escape the heat.

Emma Stone

I grew up in Arizona. I love it. I'm a part of the desert. I feel like, really, I'm from the Sonoran Desert, which is - extends to both sides of the border. I'm really from that part of Mexico, also. And I hate that there's a fence, you know, running through it.

Linda Ronstadt

And now, since I've been governor since last January, I have written numerous letters to the administration in regards to securing our borders with absolutely no response. So we have been facing this crisis, and it's devastating the people of Arizona. And I feel as governor I have a responsibility to protect the citizens.

Jan Brewer

We as governors, whether we're Republican or Democrat, we really believe that we know what's best for our people. And in Arizona, and particularly we're very interested about natural resources.

Jan Brewer

Arizona is in the midst of a fiscal crisis. We've cut school funding. And they pass a bill questioning Obama's citizenship? For real?

Kyrsten Sinema

Chicago's buoy was a couple of hundred yards astern of Arizona, and I was saddened to look at her.

Jack Adams

I love Arizona. I was raised right. Somebody has to go to Washington and knock the hell out of the place.

Ben Quayle

I enjoy playing for the Arizona Cardinals, and I want to continue to play here and try to win.

Larry Fitzgerald

No matter how many lawyers and lawsuits Obama throws at Arizona, we will have the American people and the Constitution on our side.

Russell Pearce

Arizona did not make illegal, illegal. It is a crime to enter or remain in the U.S. in violation of federal law. States have had inherent authority to enforce immigration laws when the federal government has failed or refused to do so.

Russell Pearce

In Arizona we have passed laws to free our people so that they can defend themselves and their loved ones. You cannot predict where evil will raise its head, but you can be prepared for it.

Russell Pearce

And you know, I said yesterday, you know, you know, if they're not going to - if the feds aren't going to do their job, well, then, I'm up to suing the feds to make them do their job! I mean, they sued Arizona, you know, we can sue them back! I mean, they're not - they're not enforcing the laws!

Jan Brewer

If the federal government won't secure the border, the State of Arizona will step in to complement federal efforts in a constitutional manner and protect the security of its citizens.

Jan Brewer

You know, I think there was a point in time when people didn't really understand how birth certificates were kept in the state of Hawaii, and now, I think that it's been pretty much disclosed that they used to have a long form and now they don't have a long form. Arizona used to have a long form, we now have a short form.

Jan Brewer

When I came home after my statutory term as surgeon general, I just resumed my life here in southern Arizona. Teaching at the university; my law enforcement career. Sitting on some boards. All the things I did before.

Richard Carmona

A film that I love is 'Raising Arizona' and that's funny but it's quite indie and weird and odd and quirky. I'd love to do something like that. Who knows?

Stephen Moyer

I went to prep school for one year in Arizona. It was called Orme.

Bill Kreutzmann

I'm honored to have served for 18 years as Arizona's 10th Senator - and for four terms in the House of Representatives before that.

Jon Kyl

I have long been a proponent of a guest-worker program between the United States and Mexico, and in particular I have proposed that Arizona would be an ideal location for a pilot project.

Janet Napolitano

Ensuring that high quality water is provided to all Arizona's citizens is the responsibility of elected officials at all levels and I am happy to do all I can to assist the city's efforts.

J. D. Hayworth

The notion that we won the war against Iraq is like saying we won a war against Arizona. I mean, the fact of the matter is it's not that big of a country. Nobody, I don't think, had any notion that we would do anything but win it.

Carol Moseley Braun

I grew up in Arizona and have a lot of buddies that are cowpokes.

Michael Biehn

Unfortunately, the genuine relationships and friendships that some of us have developed across the aisle in recent years does not translate into a willingness to seek compromise, consensus, or middle ground on the major challenges facing our state. The extreme ideology of the self-styled Tea Party legislators in Arizona absolutely rules the day.

Kyrsten Sinema

While I am grateful for the friendships and relationships that I have with my Republican colleagues, it would be naive to pretend that those friendships will change the way that major policies are enacted in Arizona.

Kyrsten Sinema

Arizona was the best place. I like the competition in baseball, and the football program has been great for the past five years. I think I'll be playing as a freshman in both sports, and I think I can play with them.

Terry Vaughn

But 'Hey Dude' was shot in Arizona, and that took me to the West Coast. We did 65 episodes. It was not a show that a ton of people saw, so it was like doing acting classes and getting paid for it. At that point I had the acting bug. So I went to L.A. to give it a try and never left.

Christine Taylor

'Hey Dude' was shot in Arizona, and that took me to the West Coast. We did 65 episodes. It was not a show that a ton of people saw, so it was like doing acting classes and getting paid for it. At that point I had the acting bug. So I went to L.A. to give it a try and never left.

Christine Taylor

I grew up in rural Arizona. My dad ran a general store.

Ann Kirkpatrick

The Yankees have better starting pitchers than Arizona. Arizona just has two... the Yanks have four.

Keith Hernandez

I still run into people in the business who skip over any other credits I have and say, 'I loved 'Hey, Dude!" This was back in '88, '89, '90. It was a goofy show about kids working at a dude ranch in Arizona. We did 65 episodes; I wrote 13 of them. We didn't know what we were doing, but it was writers' boot camp. It was great.

Graham Yost

I went to Phoenix, Arizona for 'Angel Unchained,' and they'd hire the bike gang from Phoenix to be extras in the movie.

Larry Bishop

In the state of Alabama we have a significant number of illegal aliens that are leaving our state as occurred in Arizona after they got tough on illegal aliens.

Mo Brooks

Senator Jon Kyl has given all of the eventual candidates in this race an excellent model of how to best serve Arizona and the country. He's set the bar extremely high, and I'll do my best to meet that standard.

Jeff Flake

I lived in Arizona, and I thought Florida was in California because I thought oranges came from the same place.

Jennifer Rubin

I didn't know much about the Mexican gray wolf before January 2011, when we contributed a flight in our Pilatus PC12 to the effort to re-establish the wolf in the forests of Arizona and New Mexico.

Joy Covey

I was ten years old in 1969, and while we lived in Arizona that year, I spent most of the summer staying with family friends in Portland, Oregon while my parents visited Spain. It was an adventure all around.

Patrick Nielsen Hayden

I was a musical theater major at the University of Arizona. And I primarily trained with Marsha Bagwell. It was a classical program, so we did Chekov and Moliere and a lot of Shakespeare.

Christine Woods